Out of Solitude

Other Books by Henri J.M. Nouwen
Published by Ave Maria Press

Behold the Beauty of the Lord
Can You Drink The Cup?
Heart Speaks to Heart
With Open Hands
Eternal Seasons, Edited by Michael Ford
The Dance of Life, Edited by Michael Ford
A Sorrow Shared

Out of Solitude

Three Meditations on the Christian Life

Henri J.M. Nouwen

ave maria press AmA notre dame, indiana

Three gospel excerpts from *The New Jerusalem Bible*, copyright © 1985, by Darton, Longman & Todd, Ltd., and Doubleday and Company, Inc.

Founded in 1865, Ave Maria Press is a ministry of the United States Province of Holy Cross.

www.avemariapress.com

ISBN-10 0-87793-495-9   ISBN-13 978-0-87793-495-0

Cover and text design by David R. Scholtes

Printed and bound in the United States of America.

Library of Congress Cataloging-in-Publication Data is available.

To Peter and Anke Naus

Contents

Foreword
by Thomas Moore

Henri Nouwen has become a beloved spiritual
writer for many people, and this book shows why.
The power of his words takes a reader off to a place in
imagination and emotion akin to a headland on the sea
or a clearing in a forest or a low peak in a range of hills.
Nouwen creates solitude with the tone and style of his
words. He evokes the very thing he is writing about.

But the simplicity of this book may be deceiving.
Nouwen makes several subtle observations, as the rhythm
and repetition of his words and phrases lull you into
reverie. Here are some of those insights that struck me.

"Nagging self-doubt is the basis of so much depression."
We're afraid, he says, that we will be unmasked and
revealed for being imperfect. We are afraid of being
judged and found wanting. Nouwen's answer echoes
the extraordinary theologian Paul Tillich: Know that you
are accepted. You are fine as who you are. Have faith in
yourself, instead of requiring approval from others, and
then get on with being connected in community.

"A life without a quiet center easily becomes destructive." Today we are especially aware of the destructive potential of human beings. Everywhere you look, on all sides of conflict, there is much action and little quiet centering. We live in a world where it is seen as pitifully passive not to act quickly and strongly, and yet Nouwen is right on track: We need a central point of stillness so that our actions are creative rather than destructive.

Henri Nouwen and I join hands in advocating care rather than cure. The compulsion to cure is like action without a deep and silent center. We want to overcome problems and adversities and want to change at all costs. An alternative is to care for ourselves, each other, and our world. We wouldn't need change and cure if we were in a constant caring mode. Even with things, today we break them and replace them. Care, in contrast, is ongoing, attentive, and from the heart. There is something heroic in cure, but parental in the best sense, artistic, and deeply compassionate about care.

But even care can "degenerate into morbid preoccupation with pain," says Nouwen. We need expectation, he says. We need to go beyond psychology.

We need a spiritual point of view. We need, finally, to discover absolute solitude and centering in God, in the full transcendence of our ego and our preoccupation with self. The final solitude is to be free of the baggage and distraction of a clamoring self, our subtle and persistent narcissism. We need to lose that particular, limiting self-consciousness in simple and ordinary contemplation.

I read this book as a highly creative and thoughtful presentation of old and tested ideas. I hear John of the Cross in the background, recommending a cleansing of the mind and the senses. I hear a fresh language charting the way toward what I would call "ordinary mysticism," the capacity in each of us to find the stillness in ourselves and in life that is the most productive place of all. The paradox is that we are most connected and most creative while living in that special kind of solitude.

Preface

These meditations were first given as sermons at "Battell," the United Church of Christ at Yale University. I am grateful to all those who helped me in the "preaching of the Word": to Phil Zaeder, the University Chaplain who invited me to the pulpit and offered his support and insight during the three weeks in his parish; to the Sisters of Mercy of Madison, Connecticut, who offered a hospitable place to write; and to the members of Battell who, by their warm reception, made me feel welcome in their midst. I also owe a special word of thanks to Joe Freeman who, with his efficient assistance, helped to prepare these sermons for publication, and to Debbie Wheeler, who gave much of her time to type and retype the manuscript.

1
OUT OF SOLITUDE

That evening, after sunset, they brought to him all who were sick and those who were possessed by devils. The whole town came crowding round the door, and he cured many who were sick with diseases of one kind or another; he also drove out many devils, but he would not allow them to speak, because they knew who he was.

In the morning, long before dawn, he got up and left the house, and went off to a lonely place and prayed there. Simon and his companions set out in search of him, and when they found him they said, "Everybody is looking for you." He answered, "Let us go elsewhere, to the neighboring country towns, so that I can proclaim the message there too, because that is why I came." And he went all through Galilee, preaching in their synagogues and driving out devils. (Mk 1:32–39)

Introduction

"In the morning, long before dawn, he got up and left the house, and went off to a lonely place and prayed there." In the middle of sentences loaded with action—healing suffering people, casting out devils, responding to impatient disciples, traveling from town to town and preaching from synagogue to synagogue—we find these quiet words: "In the morning, long before dawn, he got up and left the house, and went off to a lonely place and prayed there." In the center of breathless activities, we hear a restful breathing. Surrounded by hours of moving, we find a moment of quiet stillness. In the heart of much involvement, there are words of withdrawal. In the midst of action, there is contemplation. And after much togetherness, there is solitude. The more I read this nearly silent sentence locked in between the loud words of action, the more I have the sense that the secret of Jesus' ministry is hidden in that lonely place where he went to pray, early in the morning, long before dawn.

In the lonely place, Jesus finds the courage to follow God's will and not his own; to speak God's words and not his own; to do God's work and not his own. He reminds us constantly: "By myself I can do nothing . . . I seek to do not my own will but the will of him who sent me" (Jn 5:30). And again, "What I say to you I do not speak of my own accord: it is the Father, living in me, who is doing his works" (Jn 14:10). It is in the lonely place, where Jesus enters into intimacy with the Father, that his ministry is born.

I want to reflect on this lonely place in our lives. Somewhere we know that without a lonely place our lives are in danger. Somewhere we know that without silence words lose their meaning, that without listening speaking no longer heals, that without distance closeness cannot cure. Somewhere we know that without a lonely place our actions quickly become empty gestures. The careful balance between silence and words, withdrawal and involvement, distance and closeness, solitude and community forms the basis of the Christian life and should therefore be the subject of our most personal attention. Let us therefore look somewhat closer, first at our life in action, and then at our life in solitude.

Our Life in Action

It is not so difficult to see that, in our particular world, we all have a strong desire to accomplish something. Some of us think in terms of great dramatic changes in the structure of our society. Others want at least to build a house, write a book, invent a machine, or win a trophy. And some of us seem to be content when we just do something worthwhile for someone. But practically all of us think about ourselves in terms of our contribution to life. And when we have become old, much of our feelings of happiness or sadness depend on our evaluation of the part we played in giving shape to our world and its history. As Christians, we even feel a special call to do something good for someone: give advice, comfort, cast out a devil or two, and maybe even preach the good news from place to place.

But although the desire to be useful can be a sign of mental and spiritual health in our goal-oriented society, it can also become the source of a paralyzing lack of self-esteem. More often than not, we not only desire to do meaningful things, but we often make the results of our work the criteria of our self-esteem. And then we not only have successes, we become our successes. When you are in the habit of giving speeches in this country, you find that the older you get, the longer your introducers speak, since they feel obligated to list all your accomplishments from your college days to the present.

When we start being too impressed by the results of our work, we slowly come to the erroneous conviction that life is one large scoreboard where someone is listing the points to measure our worth. And before we are fully aware of it, we have sold our soul to the many grade-givers. That means we are not only in the world, but also of the world. Then we become what the world makes us. We are intelligent because someone gives us a high grade. We are helpful because someone says thanks. We are likable because someone likes us. And we are important because someone considers us indispensable. In short, we are worthwhile because we have successes. And the more we allow our accomplishments—the results of our actions—to become the criteria of our self-esteem, the more we are going to walk on our mental and spiritual toes, never sure if we will be able to live up to the expectations which we created by our last successes. In many people's lives, there is a nearly diabolic chain in which their anxieties grow according to their successes. This dark power has driven many of the greatest artists into self-destruction.

In this success-oriented world, our lives become more and more dominated by superlatives. We brag about the highest tower, the fastest runner, the tallest man, the longest bridge, and the best student. (In Holland we brag in reverse: we have the smallest town, the narrowest street, the tiniest house, and the most uncomfortable shoes.)

But underneath all our emphasis on successful action, many of us suffer from a deep-seated, low self-esteem and are walking around with the constant fear that someday someone will unmask the illusion and show that we are not as smart, as good, or as lovable as the world was made to believe. Once in a while, someone will confess in an intimate moment, "Everyone thinks I am very quiet and composed, but if only they knew how I really feel. . . ." This nagging self-doubt is at the basis of so much depression in the lives of many people who are struggling in our competitive society. Moreover, this corroding fear for the discovery of our weaknesses prevents community and creative sharing. When we have sold our identity to the judges of this world, we are bound to become restless, because of a growing need for affirmation and praise. Indeed, we are tempted to become low-hearted because of a constant self-rejection. And we are in serious danger of becoming isolated, since friendship and love are impossible without a mutual vulnerability.

And so, when our actions have become more an expression of fear than of inner freedom, we easily become the prisoners of our self-created illusions.

Our Life in Solitude

To live a Christian life means to live *in* the world without being *of* it. It is in solitude that this inner freedom can grow. Jesus went to a lonely place to pray, that is, to grow in the awareness that all the power he had was given to him; that all the words he spoke came from his Father; and that all the works he did were not really his, but the works of the One who had sent him. In the lonely place Jesus was made free to fail.

A life without a lonely place, that is, a life without a quiet center, easily becomes destructive. When we cling to the results of our actions as our only way of self-identification, then we become possessive and defensive and tend to look at our fellow human beings more as enemies to be kept at a distance than as friends with whom we share the gifts of life.

In solitude, we can slowly unmask the illusion of our possessiveness and discover in the center of our own self that we are not what we can conquer, but what is given to us. In solitude we can listen to the voice of him who spoke to us before we could speak a word, who healed us before we could make any gesture to help, who set us free long before we could free others, and who loved us long before we could give love to anyone. It is in this solitude that we discover that being is more important than having, and that we are worth more than the result of our efforts. In solitude we discover that our life is not a possession to be defended, but a gift to be shared. It's there we recognize that the healing words we speak are not just our own, but are given to us; that the love we can express is part of a greater love; and that the new life we bring forth is not a property to cling to, but a gift to be received.

In solitude we become aware that our worth is not the same as our usefulness. We can learn much in this respect from the old tree in the Tao story about a carpenter and his apprentice:

> A carpenter and his apprentice were walking together through a large forest. And when they came across a tall, huge, gnarled, old,

beautiful oak tree, the carpenter asked his apprentice: "Do you know why this tree is so tall, so huge, so gnarled, so old and beautiful?" The apprentice looked at his master and said:

"No . . . why?"

"Well," the carpenter said, "because it is useless. If it had been useful it would have been cut long ago and made into tables and chairs, but because it is useless it could grow so tall and so beautiful that you can sit in its shade and relax."

In solitude we can grow old freely without being preoccupied with our usefulness and we can offer a service which we had not planned on. To the degree that we have lost our dependencies on this world, whatever world means—father, mother, children, career, success or rewards—we can form a community of faith in which there is little to defend, but much to share. Because, as a community of faith, we take the world seriously, but never too seriously. In such a community, we can adopt a little of the mentality of Pope John XXIII, who could laugh about himself. When some highly decorated official asked him: "Holy Father, how many people work in the Vatican?" he paused a while and then said: "Well, I guess about half of them."

As a community of faith we work hard, but we are not destroyed by the lack of results. And as a community of faith we remind one another constantly that we form a fellowship of the weak, transparent to him who speaks to us in the lonely places of our existence and says: Do not be afraid, you are accepted.

Conclusion

"In the morning, long before dawn, he got up and left the house, and went off to a lonely place and prayed there." When Simon and his companions found him, Jesus said: "Let us go . . . to the neighboring country towns, so that I can proclaim the message there too, because that is why I came."

The words which Jesus spoke in these neighboring country towns were born in the intimacy with the Father. They were words of comfort and of condemnation, words of hope and of warning, words of unity and of division. He dared to speak these challenging words because he did not seek his own glory: "If I were to seek my own glory," he says, "my glory would be worth nothing; in fact, my glory is conferred by the Father, by the one of whom you say 'He is our God,' although you do not know him" (Jn 8:54). Within a few years, Jesus' words brought about his rejection and death. But the one who had spoken to him in the lonely place raised him up as a sign of hope and new life.

When you are able to create a lonely place in the middle of your actions and concerns, your successes and failures slowly can lose some of their power over you. For then your love for this world can merge with a compassionate understanding of its illusions. Then your serious engagement can merge with an unmasking smile. Then your concern for others can be motivated more by their needs than your own. In short: then you can care. Let us therefore live our lives to the fullest but let us not forget to once in a while get up long before dawn to leave the house and go to a lonely place.

2
WITH CARE

[Jesus and his apostles] went off in a boat to a lonely place where they could be by themselves. But people saw them going, and many recognized them; and from every town they all hurried to the place on foot and reached it before them. So as he stepped ashore he saw a large crowd; and he took pity on them because they were like sheep without a shepherd, and he set himself to teach them at some length. By now it was getting very late, and his disciples came up to him and said, "This is a lonely place and it is getting very late, so send them away, and they can go to the farms and villages round about, to buy themselves something to eat." He replied, "Give them something to eat yourselves." They answered, "Are we to go and spend two hundred denarii on bread for them to eat?" He asked, "How many loaves have you? Go and see." And when they had found out they said, "Five, and two fish." Then he ordered them to get all the people to sit down in groups on the green grass, and they sat down on the ground in squares of hundreds and fifties. Then he took the five loaves and the two fish, raised his eyes to heaven and said the blessing; then he broke the loaves and began handing them to his disciples to distribute among the people. He also shared out the two fish among them all. They all ate as much as they wanted. They collected twelve basketfuls of scraps of bread and pieces of fish. Those who had eaten the loaves numbered five thousand men. (Mk 6:32–44)

Introduction

Out of his solitude Jesus reached out his caring hand to the people in need. In the lonely place his care grew strong and mature. And from there he entered into a healing closeness with his fellow human beings.

Jesus indeed cared. Being pragmatists we say: "That is obvious: he fed the hungry, made the blind see, the deaf hear, the crippled walk, and the dead live. He indeed cared." But by being surprised by all the remarkable things he did, we forget that Jesus did not give food to the many without having received some loaves and fishes from a stranger in the crowd; that he did not return the boy of Nain to his widowed mother without having felt her sorrow; that he did not raise Lazarus from the grave without tears and a sigh of distress that came straight from the heart. What we see, and like to see, is cure and change. But what we do not see and do not want to see is care: the participation in the pain, the solidarity in suffering, the sharing in the experience of brokenness. And still, cure without care is as dehumanizing as a gift given with a cold heart.

I would like to reflect on care as the basis and precondition of all cure. In a community like ours, we have put all the emphasis on cure. We want to be professionals: heal the sick, help the poor, teach the ignorant, and organize the scattered. But the temptation is that we use our expertise to keep a safe distance from that which really matters and forget that, in the long run, cure without care is more harmful than helpful. Let us therefore first ask ourselves what care really means and then see how care can become the basis of community.

Care

What does it mean to care? Let me start by saying that the word care has become a very ambivalent word. When someone says, "I will take care of him!" it is more likely an announcement of an impending attack than of a tender compassion. And besides this ambivalence, the word care is most often used in a negative way. "Do you want coffee or tea?" "I don't care." "Do you want to stay home or go to a movie?" "I don't care." "Do you want to walk or go by car?" "I don't care." This expression of indifference toward choices in life has become commonplace. And often it seems that not to care has become more acceptable than to care, and a carefree lifestyle more attractive than a careful one.

Real care is not ambiguous. Real care excludes indifference and is the opposite of apathy. The word care finds its roots in the Gothic *Kara,* which means lament. The basic meaning of care is "to grieve, to experience sorrow, to cry out with." I am very much struck by this background of the word care because we tend to look at caring as an attitude of the strong toward the weak, of the powerful toward the powerless, of the have's toward the have-not's. And, in fact, we feel quite uncomfortable with an invitation to enter into someone's pain before doing something about it.

Still, when we honestly ask ourselves which persons in our lives mean the most to us, we often find that it is those who, instead of giving much advice, solutions, or cures, have chosen rather to share our pain and touch our wounds with a gentle and tender hand. The friend who can be silent with us in a moment of despair or confusion, who can stay with us in an hour of grief and bereavement, who can tolerate not-knowing, not-curing, not-healing and face with us the reality of our powerlessness, that is the friend who cares.

You might remember moments in which you were called to be with a friend who had lost a wife or husband, child or parent. What can you say, do, or propose at such a moment? There is a strong inclination to say: "Don't cry; the one you loved is in the hands of God." "Don't be sad because there are so many good things left worth living for." But are we ready to really experience our powerlessness in the face of death and say: "I do not understand. I do not know what to do, but I am here with you." Are we willing to *not* run away from the pain, to *not* get busy when there is nothing to do, and instead stand in the face of death together with those who grieve?

The friend who cares makes it clear that whatever happens in the external world, being present to each other is what really matters. In fact, it matters more than pain, illness, or even death. It is remarkable how much consolation and hope we can receive from authors who, while offering no answers to life's questions, have the courage to articulate the situation of their lives in all honesty and directness. Kierkegaard, Sartre, Camus, Hammarskjöld, and Merton: none of them have ever offered solutions. Yet many of us who have read their works have found new strength to pursue our own search. Their courage to enter so deeply into human suffering and to become present to their own pain gave them the power to speak healing words.

Therefore, to care means first of all to be present to each other. From experience, you know that those who care for you become present to you. When they listen, they listen to you. When they speak, you know they speak to you. And when they ask questions, you know it is for your sake and not for their own. Their presence is a healing presence because they accept you on your terms, and they encourage you to take your own life seriously and to trust your own vocation.

Our tendency is to run away from the painful realities or to try to change them as soon as possible. But cure without care makes us into rulers, controllers, manipulators, and prevents a real community from taking shape. Cure without care makes us preoccupied with quick changes, impatient and unwilling to share each other's burden. And so cure can often become offending instead of liberating. It is therefore not so strange that cure is not seldom refused by people in need. Not only have individuals refused help when they did not sense a real care, but also oppressed minorities have resisted support, and suffering nations have declined medicine and food when they realized that it was better to suffer than to lose self-respect by accepting a gift out of a non-caring hand.

Community and Care

This leaves us with the urgent question: How can we be or become a caring community, a community of people not trying to cover the pain or to avoid it by sophisticated bypasses, but rather to share it as the source of healing and new life? It is important to realize that you cannot get a Ph.D. in caring, that caring cannot be delegated by specialists, and that therefore nobody can be excused from caring. Still, in a society like ours, we have a strong tendency to refer to specialists. When someone does not feel well, we quickly think, "Where can we find a doctor?" When someone is confused, we easily advise him to go to a counselor. And when someone is dying, we quickly call a priest. Even when someone wants to pray we wonder if there is a minister around.

> That was also the case two centuries ago in June 1787 during the days of deliberation about the Constitution of the United States. When the discussions did not seem to get

anywhere, Benjamin Franklin proposed to open the sessions with prayer. But the delegation to the convention rejected the proposal not because they did not believe in prayer but because they had no money to pay a chaplain. (S. E. Morrison, *The Oxford History of the American People*. New York, 1965, pp. 307–308)

Although it is usually very meaningful to call on outside help, sometimes our referral to others is more a sign of fear to face the pain than a sign of care, and in that case we keep our greatest gift to heal hidden from each other. Every human being has a great, yet often unknown, gift to care, to be compassionate, to become present to the other, to listen, to hear and to receive. If that gift would be set free and made available, miracles could take place. Those who really can receive bread from a stranger and smile in gratitude, can feed many without even realizing it. Those who can sit in silence with their fellow man, not knowing what to say, but knowing that they should be there, can bring new life in a dying heart. Those who are not afraid to hold a hand in gratitude, to shed tears in grief, and to let a sigh of distress arise straight from the heart, can break through paralyzing boundaries and witness the birth of a new fellowship, the fellowship of the broken.

Why is it that we keep that great gift of care so deeply hidden? Why is it that we keep giving dimes without daring to look into the face of the beggar? Why is it that we do not join the lonely eater in the dining hall but look for those we know so well? Why is it that we so seldom knock on a door or grab a phone, just to say hello, just to show that we have been thinking about each other? Why are smiles still hard to get and words of comfort so difficult to come by? Why is it so hard to express thanks to a teacher, admiration to a student, and appreciation to the men and women who cook, clean, and garden? Why do we keep bypassing each other always on the way to something or someone more important?

Maybe simply because we ourselves are so concerned with being different from the others that we do not even allow ourselves to lay down our heavy armor and come together in a mutual vulnerability. Maybe we are so full of our own opinions, ideas, and convictions that we have no space left to listen to the other and learn from him or her.

> There is a story about a university professor who came to a Zen master to ask him about Zen. Nan-in, the Zen master, served him tea. He poured his visitor's cup full, and then kept pouring. The professor watched the overflow until he could no longer restrain himself. "It is over-full. No more will go in!" "Like this cup," Nan-in said, "You are full of your own opinions and speculations. How can I teach you Zen unless you first empty your cup?"

To care means first of all to empty our own cup and to allow the other to come close to us. It means to take away the many barriers which prevent us from entering into communion with the other. When we dare to care, then we discover that nothing human is foreign to us, but that all the hatred and love, cruelty and compassion, fear and joy can be found in our own hearts. When we dare to care, we have to confess that when others kill, I could have killed too. When others torture, I could have done the same. When others heal, I could have healed too. And when others give life, I could have done the same. Then we experience that we can be present to the soldier who kills, to the guard who pesters, to the young man who plays as if life has no end, and to the old man who stopped playing out of fear of death.

By the honest recognition and confession of our human sameness we can participate in the care of God who came, not to the powerful but to the powerless, not to be different but to be the same, not to take our pain away but to share it. Through this participation, we can open our hearts to each other and form a new community.

Conclusion

When Jesus had received five loaves and two fishes, he returned them to the crowd, and there was plenty for all to eat. The gift is born out of receiving. Food came forth out of kinship with the hungry, healing out of compassion, cure out of care. He or she who can cry out with those in need can give without offense.

As long as we are occupied and preoccupied with our desire to do good but are not able to feel the crying need of those who suffer, our help remains hanging somewhere between our minds and our hands and does not descend into the heart where we can care. But in solitude, our heart can slowly take off its many protective devices, and can grow so wide and deep that nothing human is strange to it.

Then we can become contrite, crushed, and broken, not just by our own sins and failings, but also by the pain of our fellow human beings. Then we can give birth to a new awareness reaching far beyond the boundaries of our human efforts. And then we who, in our fearful narrow-mindedness, were afraid that we would not have enough food for ourselves, will have to smile. For then we will discover that, after having fed more than five thousand, there were still twelve baskets of bread and fish remaining. Then our care born out of solitude can become a sign of our faithful expectation of the coming day of complete joy.

3
IN EXPECTATION

[On the night that he was betrayed, Jesus said to his apostles:] "In a short time you will no longer see me, and then a short time later you will see me again."

Then some of his disciples said to one another, "What does he mean, 'In a short time you will no longer see me, and then a short time later you will see me again'? . . . What is this 'short time'? We don't know what he means." Jesus knew that they wanted to question him, so he said, "You are asking one another what I meant by saying, 'In a short time you will no longer see me, and then a short time later you will see me again.'

"In all truth I tell you, you will be weeping and wailing while the world will rejoice; you will be sorrowful, but your sorrow will turn to joy. A woman in childbirth suffers, because her time has come; but when she has given birth to the child she forgets the suffering in her joy that a human being has been born into the world.

So it is with you: you are sad now, but I shall see you again, and your hearts will be full of joy, and that joy no one shall take from you." (Jn 16:16–22)

Introduction

Care born out of solitude can hardly last unless undergirded by a hopeful expectation for the day of fulfillment when God will be all in all. Without expectation, care easily degenerates into a morbid preoccupation with pain and gives more occasion for common complaints than for the formation of community. But Jesus sets us free from self-complaint by pointing beyond the short time of care to the great day of joy.

"In a short time you will no longer see me, and then a short time later you will see me again. . . . You are sad now, but . . . your hearts will be full of joy, and that joy no one shall take from you."

Our life is a short time in expectation, a time in which sadness and joy kiss each other at every moment. There is a quality of sadness that pervades all the moments of our life. It seems that there is no such thing as clear-cut pure joy, but that, even in the most happy moments of our existence, we sense a tinge of sadness. In every satisfaction, there is an awareness of its limitations. In every success, there is the fear of jealousy. Behind every smile, there is a tear. In every embrace, there is loneliness. In every friendship, distance. And in all forms of light, there is the knowledge of surrounding darkness.

Joy and sadness are as close to each other as the splendid colored leaves of a New England fall to the soberness of the barren trees. When you touch the hand of a returning friend, you already know that he will have to leave you again. When you are moved by the quiet vastness of a sun-covered ocean, you miss the friend who cannot see the same. Joy and sadness are born at the same time, both arising from such deep places in your heart that you can't find words to capture your complex emotions.

But this intimate experience in which every bit of life is touched by a bit of death can point us beyond the limits of our existence. It can do so by making us look forward in expectation to the day when our hearts will be filled with perfect joy, a joy that no one shall take away from us. Let me therefore now reflect on expectation, first about expectation as patience, and then about expectation as joy.

Expectation as Patience

The mother of expectation is patience. The French author Simone Weil writes in her notebooks: "Waiting patiently in expectation is the foundation of the spiritual life." Without patience, our expectation degenerates into wishful thinking. Patience comes from the word *patior* which means, "to suffer." The first thing that Jesus promises is suffering: "I tell you, you will be weeping and wailing . . . and you will be sorrowful." But he calls these pains birth pains. And so, what seems a hindrance becomes a way; what seems an obstacle becomes a door; what seems a misfit becomes a cornerstone. Jesus changes our history from a random series of sad incidents and accidents into a constant opportunity for a change of heart. To wait patiently therefore means to allow our weeping and wailing to become the purifying preparation by which we are made ready to receive the joy which is promised to us.

A few years ago I met an old professor at the University of Notre Dame. Looking back on his long life of teaching, he said with a funny twinkle in his eyes, "I have always been complaining that my work was constantly interrupted, until I slowly discovered that my interruptions were my work."

That is the great conversion in our life: to recognize and believe that the many unexpected events are not just disturbing interruptions of our projects, but the way in which God molds our hearts and prepares us for his return. Our great temptations are boredom and bitterness. When our good plans are interrupted by poor weather, our well-organized careers by illness or bad luck, our peace of mind by inner turmoil, our hope for peace by a new war, our desire for a stable government by a constant changing of the guards, and our desire for immortality by real death, we are tempted to give in to a paralyzing boredom or to strike back in destructive bitterness. But when we believe that patience can make our expectations grow, then fate can be converted into a vocation, wounds into a call for deeper understanding, and sadness into a birthplace of joy.

I would like to tell you the story of a middle-aged man whose career was suddenly interrupted by the discovery of leukemia, a fatal blood cancer. All his life plans crumbled, and all his ways had to change. But slowly he was able to ask himself no longer, "Why did this happen to me? What did I do wrong to deserve this fate?" but instead, "What is the promise hidden in this event?" When his rebellion became a new quest, he felt that he could give strength and hope to other cancer patients and that, by facing his condition directly, he could make his pain into a source of healing for others. To this day, this man not only does more for patients than many ministers are able to do, but he also refound his life on a level that he had never known before.

Expectation as Joy

Whereas patience is the mother of expectation, it is expectation itself that brings new joy to our lives. Jesus not only made us look at our pains, but also beyond them. "You are sad now, but I shall see you again, and your hearts will be full of joy." A man or a woman without hope in the future cannot live creatively in the present. The paradox of expectation indeed is that those who believe in tomorrow can better live today, that those who expect joy to come out of sadness can discover the beginnings of a new life in the center of the old, that those who look forward to the returning Lord can discover him already in their midst.

You know how a letter can change your day. When you watch people in front of the wall of mailboxes, you can see how a small piece of paper can change the expression on a face, can make a curved back straight, and a sullen mouth whistle again. The day might be just as dull as the day before and the work just as tiring. But the letter in your mailbox telling you that someone loves you, that someone is looking forward to meeting you again, that someone needs your presence, or that someone promises to come soon, makes all the difference.

A life lived in expectation is like a life in which we have received a letter, a letter which makes him whom we have missed so much return even earlier than we could imagine. Expectation brings joy to the center of our sadness and the loved one to the heart of our longings. The one who stayed with us in the past and will return to us in the future becomes present to us in that precious moment in which memory and hope touch each other. At that moment we can realize that we can only expect someone because he has already touched us. A student from California who had to leave many of his good friends behind to come to school at the faraway East Coast recently said to me: "It was hard to depart; but if the good-bye is not painful, the hello cannot be joyful either." And so his sadness of September became his joy at Christmas time.

Is God present or is he absent? Maybe we can say now that in the center of our sadness for his absence we can find the first signs of his presence. And that, in the middle of our longings, we discover the footprints of the one who has created them. It is in the faithful waiting for the loved one that we know how much he has filled our lives already. Just as the love of a mother for her son can grow while she is waiting for his return, and just as lovers can rediscover each other during long periods of absence, so also our intimate relationship with God can become deeper and more mature while we wait patiently in expectation for his return.

Conclusion

"In a short time you will no longer see me, and then a short time later you will see me again." We are living in this short time. We can live in it creatively when we live it out of solitude, i.e., detached from the results of our work. And when we live it with care, i.e., crying with those who weep and wail. But it is the expectation of his return which molds our solitude and care into a preparation for the day of great joy.

This is what we express when we take bread and wine in thanksgiving. We do not eat bread to still our hunger or drink wine to quench our thirst. We just eat a little bit of bread and drink a little bit of wine, in the realization that God's presence is the presence of the One who came, but is still to come; who touched our hearts, but has not yet taken all our sadness away.

And so when we share some bread and some wine together, we do this not as people who have arrived, but as men and women who can support each other in patient expectation until we see him again. And then our hearts will be full of joy, a joy that no one can take away from us.

Henri J.M. Nouwen is one of the most popular spiritual writers of our time. He wrote more than forty books, among them the best-selling *Can You Drink the Cup?* and *With Open Hands*. He taught at the University of Notre Dame, as well as Yale and Harvard Universities. From 1986 until his death in 1996, he was part of the L'Arche Daybreak community in Toronto where he shared his life with people with developmental disabilities. For additional information on the life of Henri Nouwen visit www.henrinouwen.org.